ABOUT US

YesWeCode is much more than just a program; it is an initiative of Hakili Community for Sustainable Development, a registered Canadian charity (769649112RR0001), dedicated to the development of children and the future of our society.

At YesWeCode, we believe that every child deserves to develop the skills necessary to navigate the digital world of tomorrow. Through our pre-coding activity book, we provide young minds from all backgrounds with the tools to dream big and build a future full of possibilities.

Together, we can shape a world where every child, regardless of their background, has the chance to discover the magic of technology and become a change-maker. Join us in this mission.

For more info. visit: https://www.yeswecode.ca/

Since 2019

- Over 200 meaningful learning experience
- More than 50 volunteers involved and trained
- Nearly 5,000 hours of programming lessons delivered

INDEX

CONCEPTS	PAGE
1. Sequence	4-8
2. Decomposition	9-13
3. Repetition	14-17
4. Pattern recognition	18-22
5. Conditional Statements	23-24
6. How can you support us	25

Welcome to the exciting world of pre-coding! This book is your passport to a journey filled with puzzles, creativity, and problem-solving.

Each activity you find here is a step that will help your child become a true coding wizard. Get ready to explore mazes that will challenge their logical thinking, colouring activities that will stimulate their imagination and puzzles that will make them think like programmers.

By completing these activities, your child will have fun while developing essential skills to understand the magic of coding. So, grab your crayons, put on your thinking cap, and embark on this incredible adventure together!

PUT IN ORDER

Computers are like simple machines. They don't automatically know which command comes first or next. As coders, it's our job to guide them. Arranging the steps in the correct order helps the computer complete tasks quickly and reach its target. The fancy word for it is sequencing.

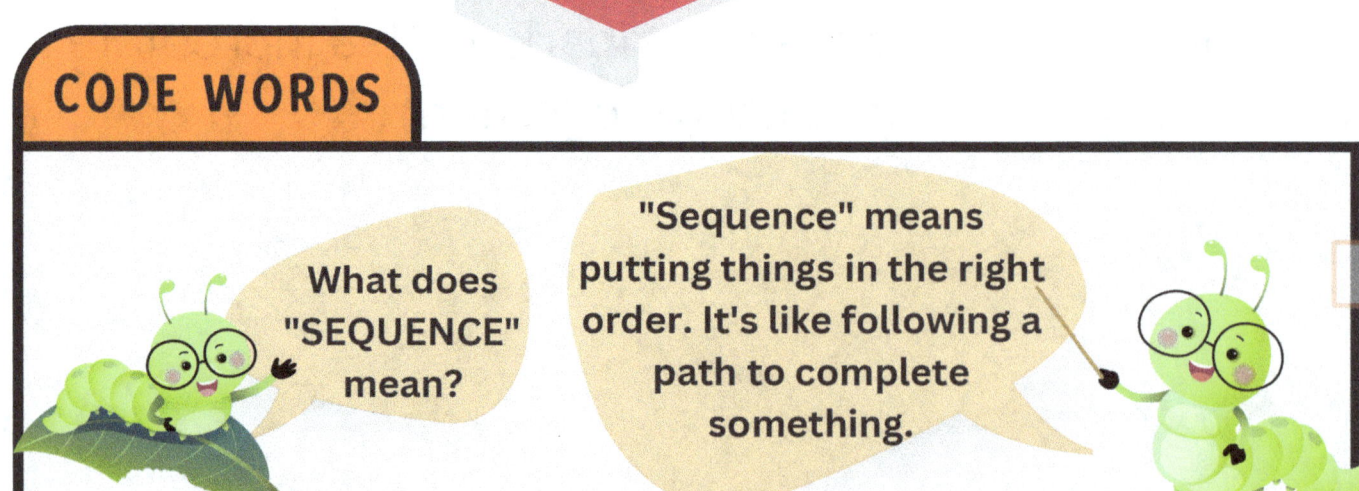

CODE WORDS

What does "SEQUENCE" mean?

"Sequence" means putting things in the right order. It's like following a path to complete something.

SEQUENCING ACTIVITY 1

Can you help the baby monkey reach the bananas?

Cut and paste the arrows in the correct sequence.

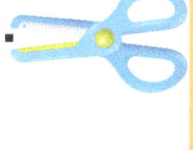

SEQUENCING ACTIVITY 2

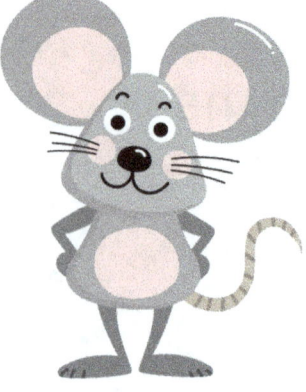

Can you help the baby mouse reach the cheese? Cut and paste the arrows in the correct sequence.

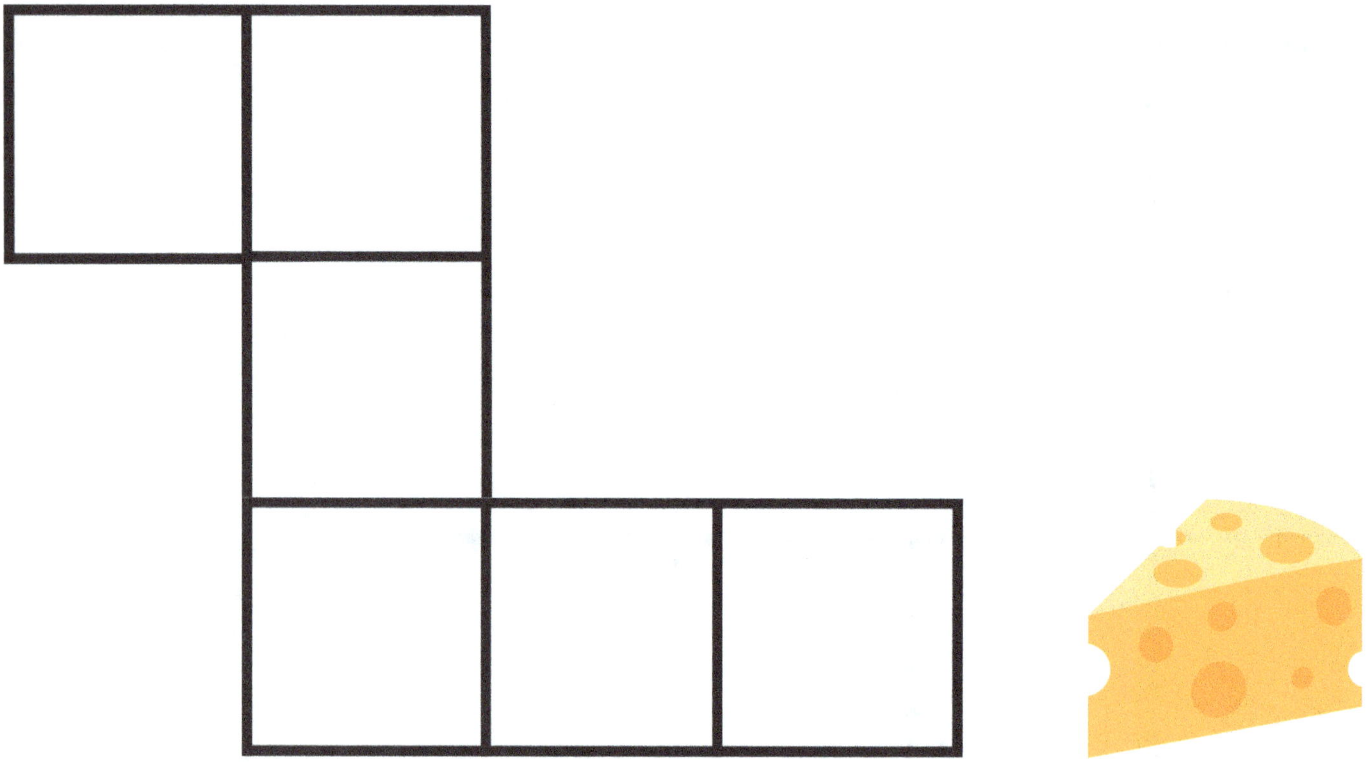

{YesWeCode}
kids coding like pros

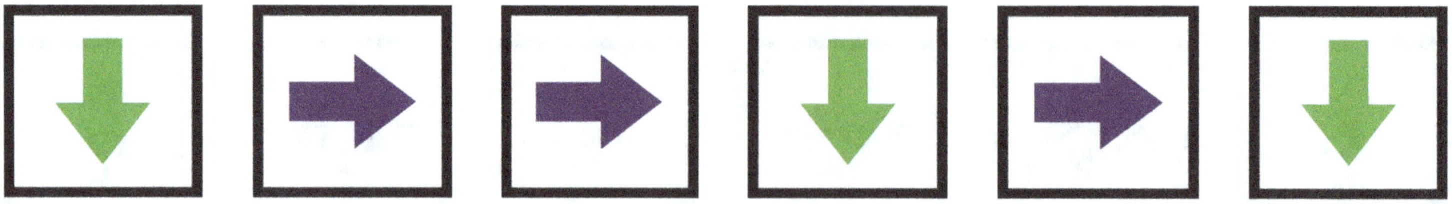

SEQUENCING ACTIVITY 3

Can you help the baby frog reach the lily pad?
Cut and paste the arrows in the correct sequence.

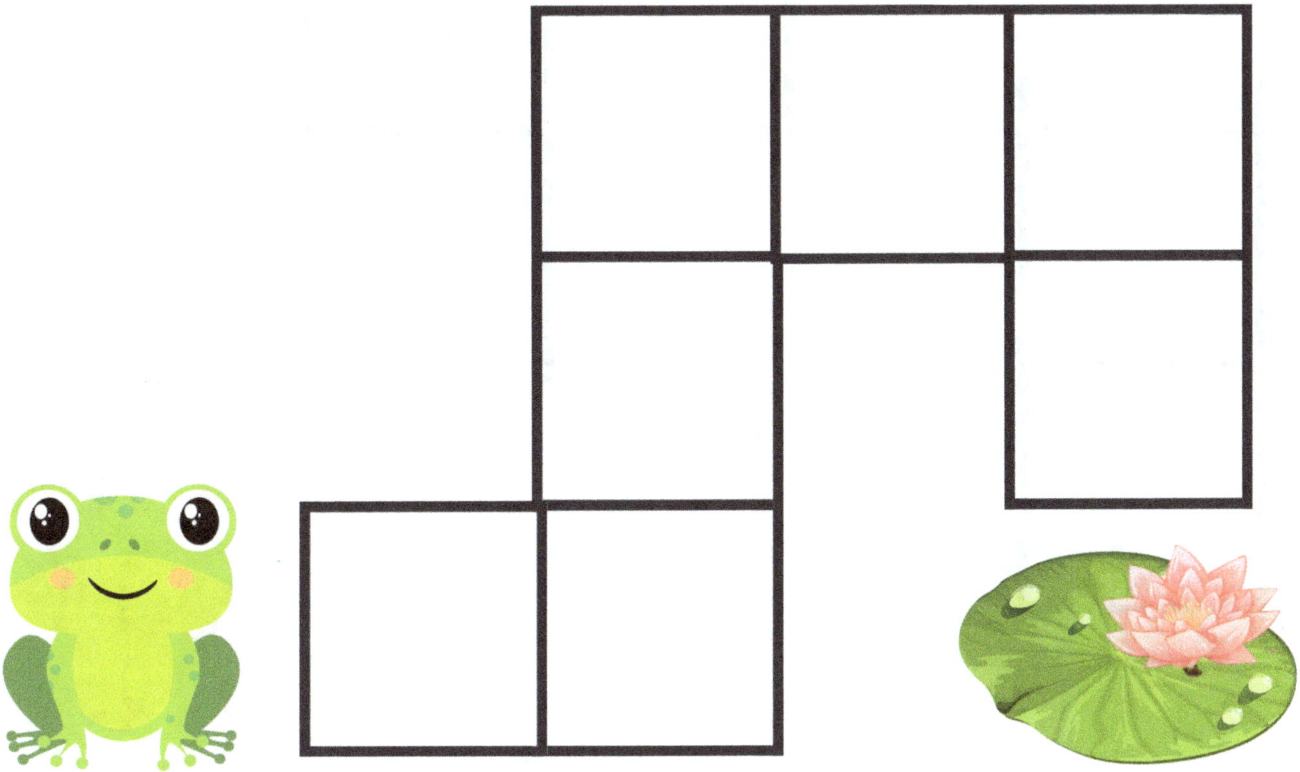

{YesWeCode}
kids coding like pros

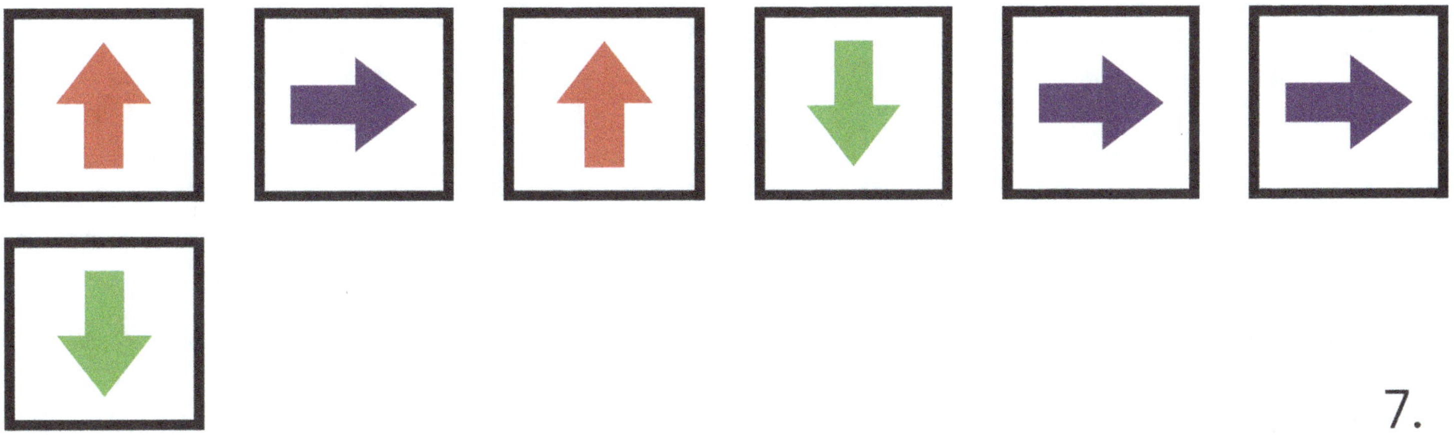

SEQUENCING ACTIVITY 4

Can you help the baby alien reach the UFO?
Cut and paste the arrows in the correct sequence.

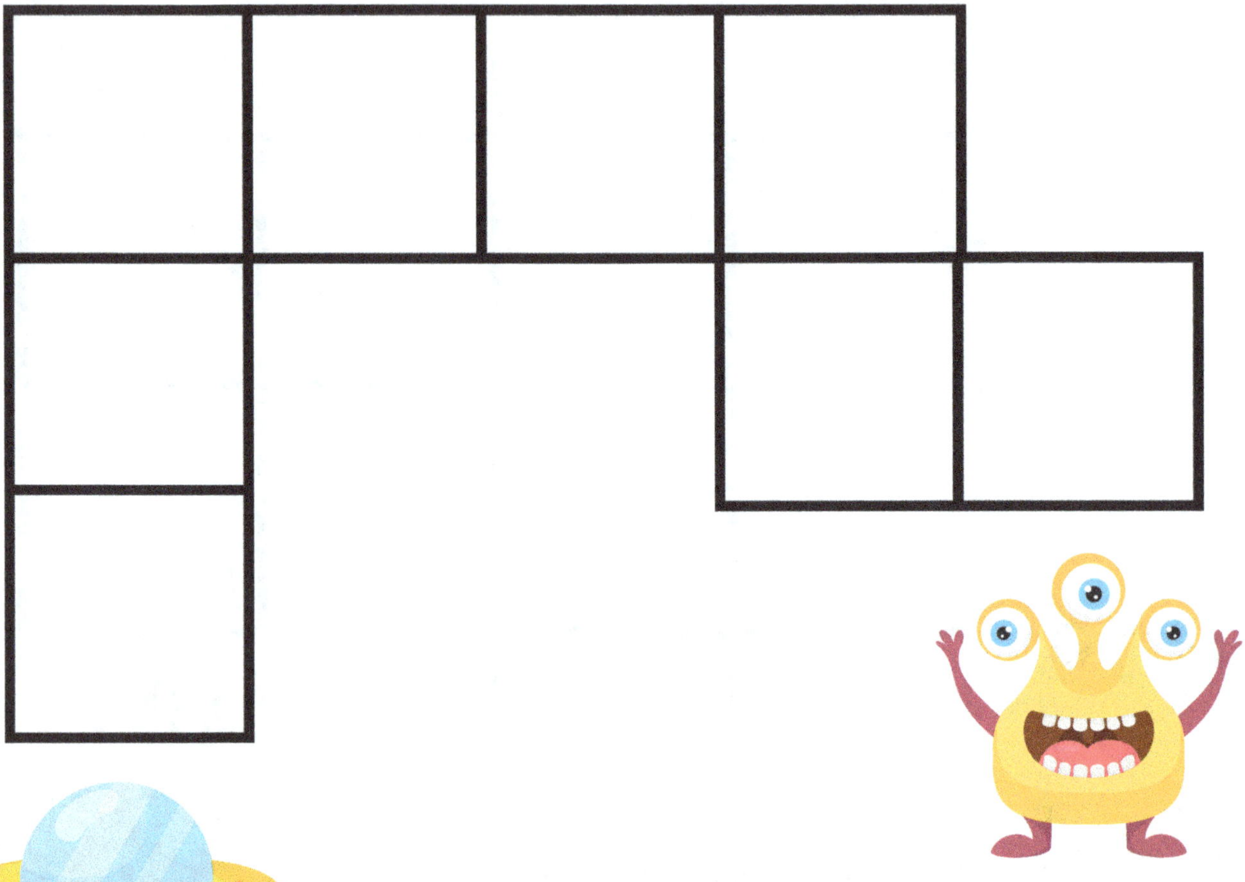

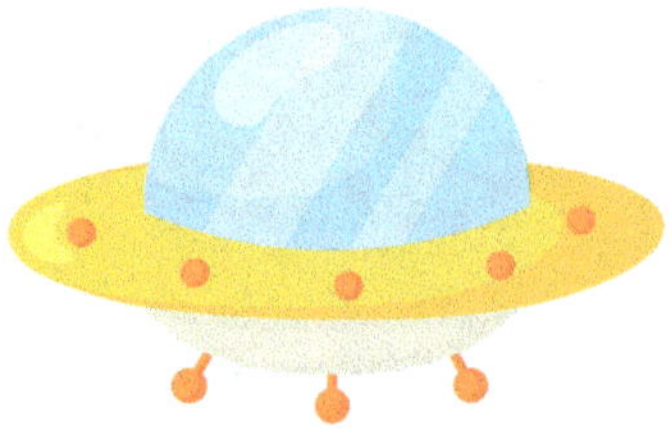

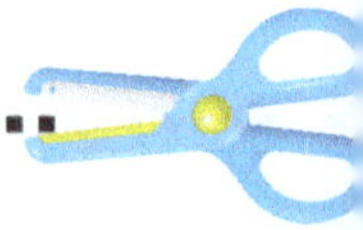

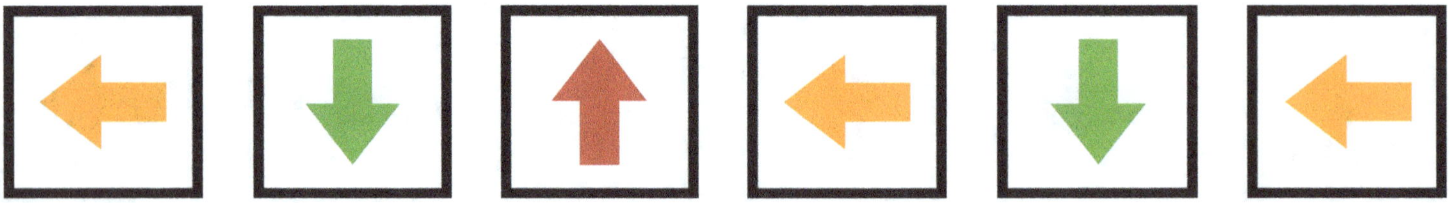

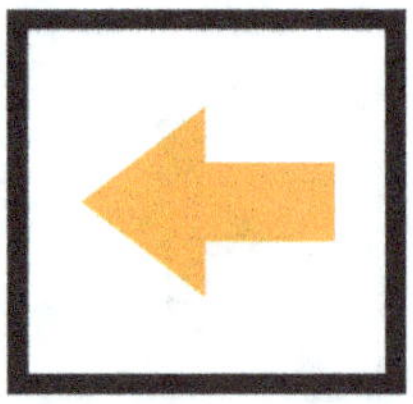

BREAK IT DOWN

In computer science, we encounter complex problems, a bit like puzzles, that we want to solve. Breaking these big problems into smaller parts makes it easier to understand and solve them. The fancy word for it is decomposition.

CODE WORDS

What does "DECOMPOSE" mean?

"Decompose" means to take apart something big and make it into smaller, more manageable parts.
It's like breaking a big problem into little pieces to understand and solve it.

DECOMPOSITION ACTIVITY 1

How many squares, triangles, circles, and rectangles do you see? Could you write the number in the corresponding boxes below?

10.

DECOMPOSITION ACTIVITY 2

How many squares, triangles, circles, and rectangles do you see? Could you write the number in the corresponding boxes below?

DECOMPOSITION ACTIVITY 3

How many squares, triangles, circles, and rectangles do you see? Could you write the number in the corresponding boxes below?

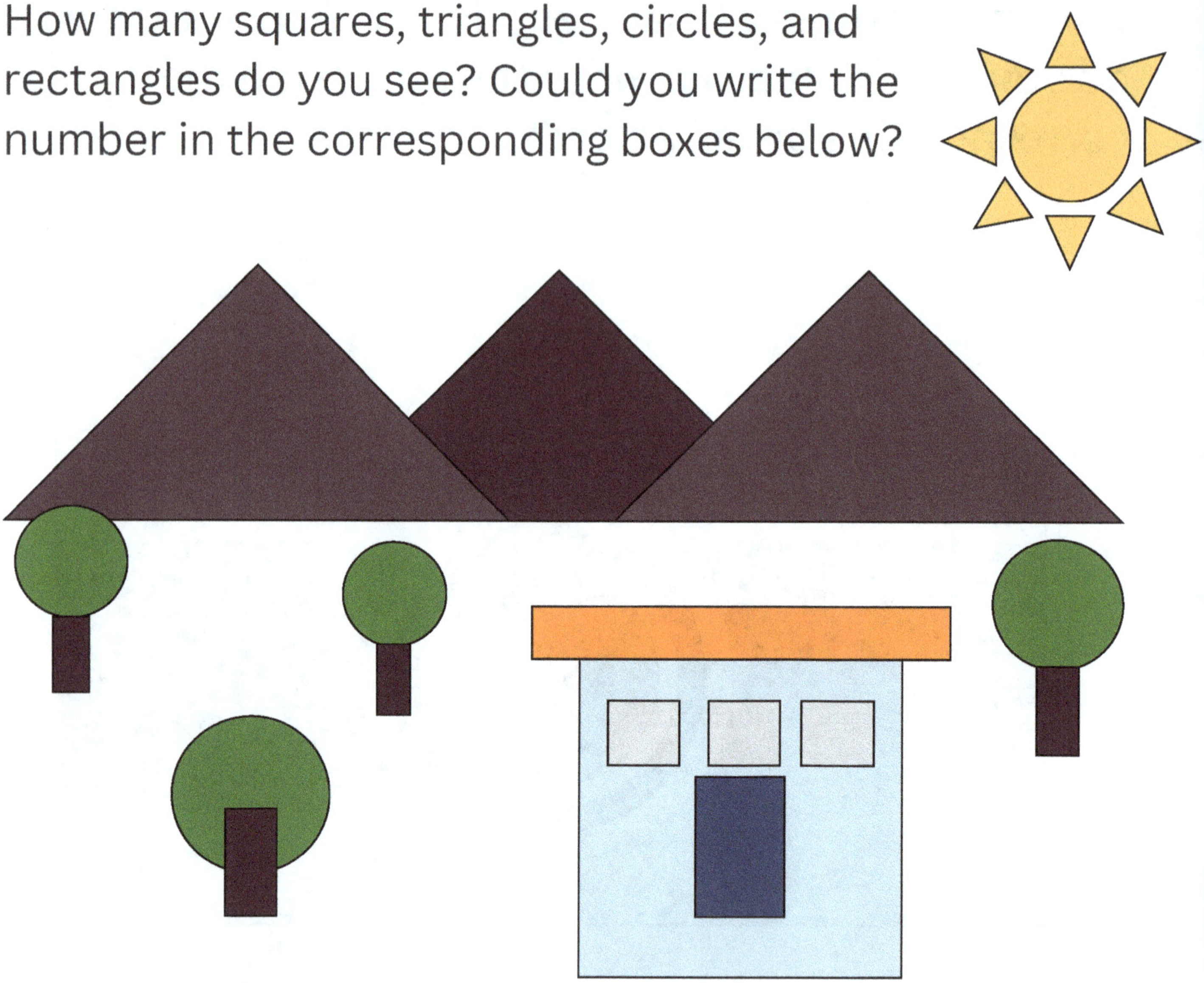

DECOMPOSITION ACTIVITY 4

How many squares, triangles, circles, and rectangles do you see? Could you write the number in the corresponding boxes below?

13.

REPETITION

Sometimes we need to tell a computer to repeat a task. It is helpful because it helps us save time and simplify things. Instead of writing the exact instruction many times, we can tell the computer to repeat the instruction until something specific happens. Therefore, we can ask the computer to do a task on its own without us having to keep saying it. The fancy word for it is loop.

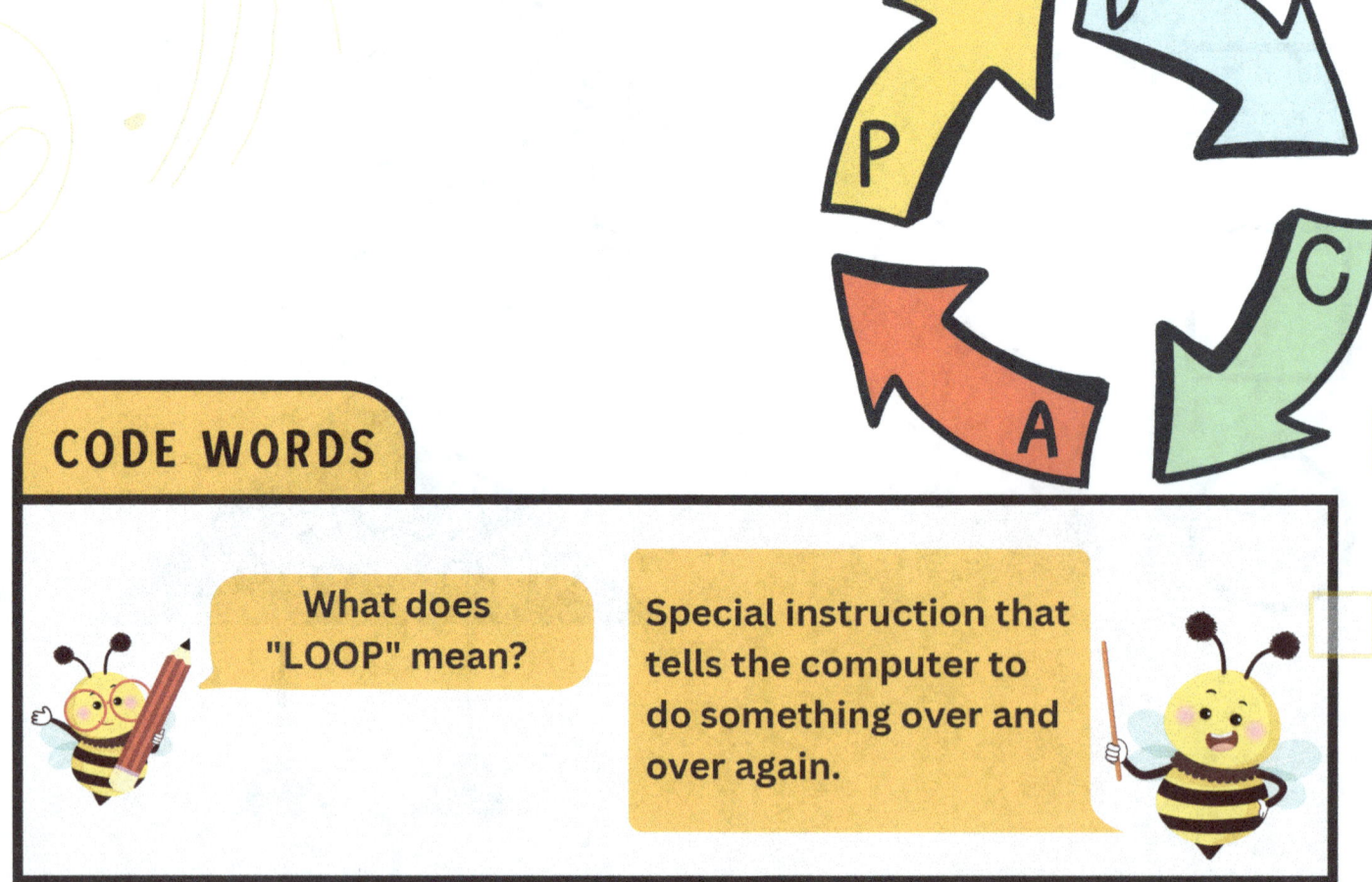

CODE WORDS

What does "LOOP" mean?

Special instruction that tells the computer to do something over and over again.

REPETITION ACTIVITY 1

Can you count how many cupcakes still need frosting to finish the level? Write the number in the circle.

So we need to repeat the **Frosting Task** times in a loop to finish the level.

REPETITION ACTIVITY 2

Let's count how many berries we need to pick to finish the level. Can you write the number in the circle?

So, we need to repeat the **Picking Berry Task** times in a loop to finish the Level.

REPETITION ACTIVITY 3

Let's count how many times we need to drop the fishing rod to catch all the fish and finish the level! Can you write the number in the circle?

So, we need to repeat the **Fishing Task** times in loop to finish the Level.

PATTERN RECOGNITION

Pattern recognition is like playing a game where you look for things that repeat. For example, if you always see colors like red, blue, red, blue, you notice a pattern. In programming, it's a bit the same! For example, if we always see a sequence of numbers, we can know which number comes next. It's like following a recipe or pattern to do something in an organized and predictable way. So recognizing patterns helps computers understand how to do things correctly, just like you find patterns in your games or drawings.

CODE WORDS

What is " PATTERN RECOGNITION" for?

By recognizing patterns, computers can solve problems, follow sequences of instructions, and repeat tasks efficiently

CONNECT THE DOTS ACTIVITY 1

Connect the dots in the correct order and use your favourite colors to bring the rocket to life.

19.

CONNECT THE DOTS ACTIVITY 2

Connect the dots in the correct order and use your favourite colours to bring the robot to life.

{YesWeCode}
kids coding like pros

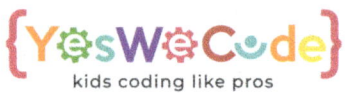

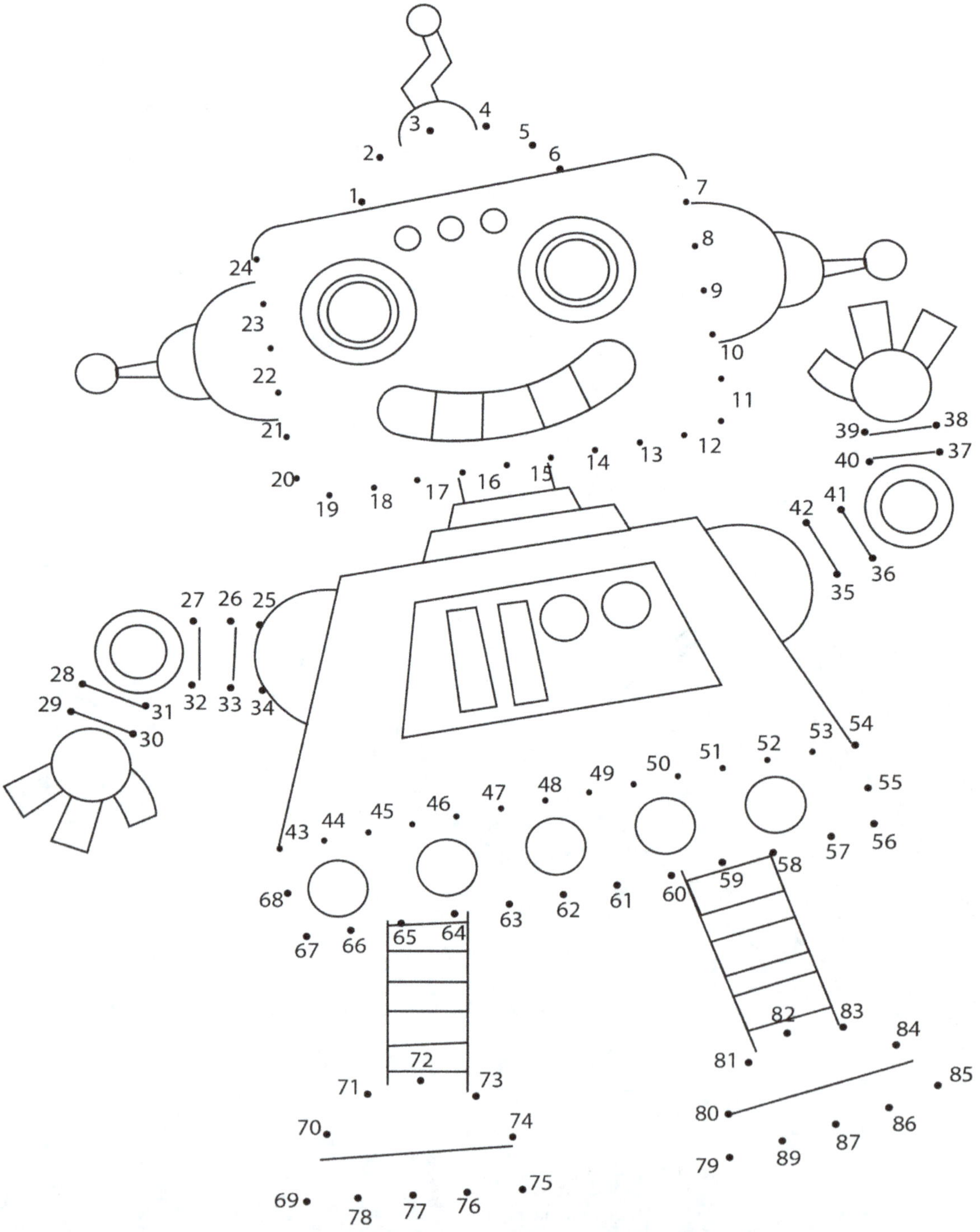

COLOURING BY NUMBER ACTIVITY 1

21.

COLOURING BY NUMBER ACTIVITY 2

							1	1			
							2	1	1		
							2	2	1	1	
							2	2	2	1	1
							2	2	2	2	1	1
							3	3	2	2	2	1
							4	3	2	2	2	
							3	3	2	2	2	
							2	2	2	2	2	
							2	2	2	2	2	
							5	5	5	5	5	5

1 (brown) 2 (yellow) 3 (dark brown) 4 (light blue) 5 (black)

22.

CONDITIONAL STATEMENTS

Imagine that you are in a maze with several paths. At each crossroads, you have to choose whether you go left or right. This is exactly how computers work! They use conditional statements to make decisions. They analyze a situation, just like you in the maze, and choose the direction to follow.

Branches, or conditional statements, are like intersections in a maze where the computer decides which path to take based on what it "sees."

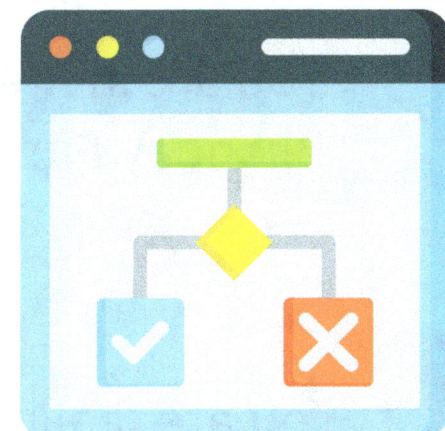

CODE WORDS

What is "BRANCHING" for?

Branching means creating conditions or choices for a computer to decide what action to take based on the situation.

CONDITIONAL STATEMENT ACTIVITY

Connect the pictures by drawing a line to match the "if" and "then" statements.

IF...   THEN...

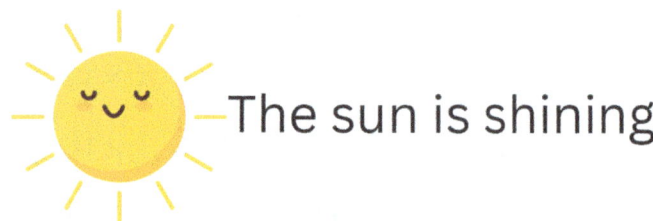 The sun is shining

Its time to go to bed.

 You are invited to a Birthday Party

We will play outside.

 You are feeling tired

Its time to wake up.

 The alarm rings

You should bring a gift.

SUPPORT US

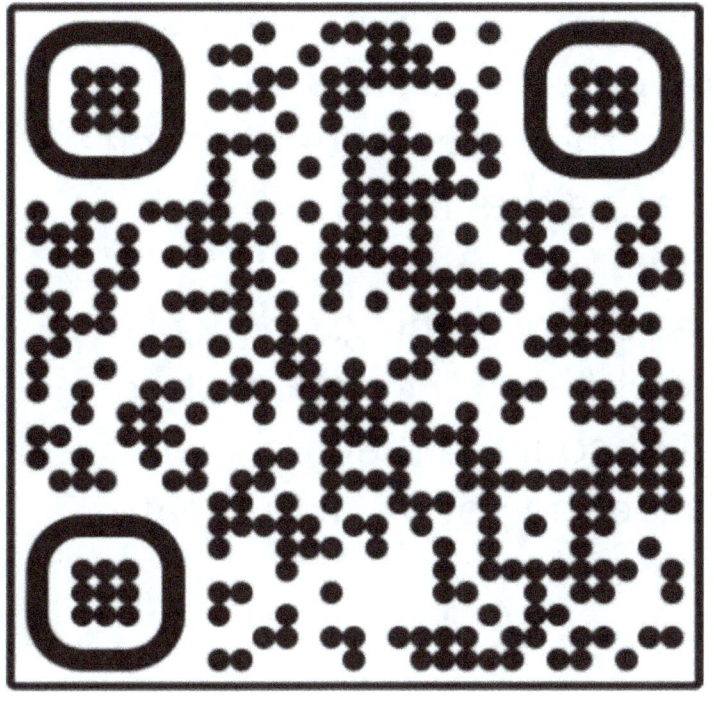

If you enjoyed the activities in this book and would like us to continue offering our program free to families, you can support us by purchasing other resources or making a donation to our program.

Make a donation by scanning the QR code and receive a tax receipt

Your small actions can have a big impact

Congratulations on completing this introductory programming activity book! Your child has explored mazes, coloured characters, and solved puzzles like a true programmer. We hope you enjoyed these activities as much as we enjoyed creating them.

The skills developed here are just the beginning. Coding is like solving digital puzzles; your child is on the right path to becoming a great programmer! Encourage them to keep exploring and imagining – they have the potential to create amazing things.

Thank you for joining us on this adventure. Your child's curiosity and determination make learning so exciting. Keep supporting them, and remember that they can turn their ideas into reality.

Stay curious and never stop learning! Your child is a coding champion in the making, and we can't wait to see all they will accomplish.

Happy coding, and keep reaching for the stars!